Original title:
Where Gratitude Meets Generosity

Copyright © 2024 Creative Arts Management OÜ
All rights reserved.

Author: Rosalie Bradford
ISBN HARDBACK: 978-9916-94-328-1
ISBN PAPERBACK: 978-9916-94-329-8

A Heartfelt Mosaic

In a garden of thank-yous, I plant a seed,
Watering with laughter, my heart's a good deed.
A smile grows like wildflowers, bursting with cheer,
Sharing pies, and giggles, making friends near.

With a wink and a nudge, generosity blooms,
As I toss confetti, laughter fills the rooms.
A parade of warm wishes, twirling with glee,
Like a silly sock puppet, dancing free.

Who knew that kindness could come in a dance?
Twisting and turning, I'll give it a chance.
A hat made of gratitude, perched on my head,
Makes everyone chuckle, not a single dread.

So let's bake a cake with sprinkles galore,
Where friendship and laughter twirl 'round the floor.
With each slice of joy, we pass it around,
In this funny mosaic, love's joy can be found.

Gratitude's Gracious Touch

A thank-you note, I designed with glee,
It said 'you rock, and way more than me!'
But when it arrived, to my pure dismay,
The postman commented, 'What a quirky bouquet!'

My cat's been gifted a grand ribbon roll,
She's wrapped it round like a baseball goal.
I thanked my friend, but she just rolled her eyes,
Said 'you might just out-fool a pack of wise guys.'

The Well of Abundance

In my backyard lies a well so deep,
Filled with trinkets I no longer keep.
I toss in my gripes, like coins in a slot,
Then fish out a laugh—it's a whimsical plot!

My neighbor drops by with cookies in hand,
I thought they were pancakes, the size of a land.
'Grateful for treats?' I said, with a grin,
'Please share the recipe, did you toss it in the bin?'

Gifting in Silence

A secret gift, wrapped up with a bow,
But inside it's just onions, as you might know.
My friend took a sniff and burst into tears,
Although I was silent, my intent was quite clear!

I dropped off some socks, a fine pair so warm,
But they were striped, and failed to charm.
He said with a laugh, 'Thanks, my colorful mate,
Now I can wear them on an entirely new date!'

Harmony of Heartfelt Acts

A dance of kindness, a twirl and a spin,
We share our delights with a giggle and grin.
But when I fell flat, in the middle of toast,
My friends rolled with laughter, they loved it the most!

A round of good deeds, we geo-tagged in fun,
But mistook the GPS, led us to none.
Yet we found a good bakery, a sweet happy stop,
Where we gifted our hearts and couldn't quite drop!

Radiant Threads of Togetherness

In a world of clashing socks,
We share our mismatched flair.
With laughs that fill the air,
Who knew odd pairs could care?

A pie that's half burnt, it's true,
Still tastes like pure delight.
We pass it round with glee,
And toast to every bite!

The Blessing of Shared Abundance

A basket full of veggies bright,
We fight for who gets peas.
Lettuce dons a silly hat,
While we share all our keys.

Each cookie's baked with love,
But one's a bit too stiff.
We laugh and then we share,
Till crumbs become a gift!

The Glow of Unspoken Thanks

A nod, a grin, a silly wink,
That's all we need to say.
With hearts that dance like jellybeans,
We brighten up the day.

You brought me tea, I spilled it here,
Now that's a perfect blend.
A toast to chaos, please, my friend,
Where fun will never end!

Acts Woven with Care

A sweater knitted with a flaw,
Is worn with such great pride.
It warms the heart to see it,
Thus wears our humor wide.

The coffee pot makes quite the mess,
But sharing spills is fun.
So raise a cup to fumbles,
For laughter's just begun!

An Oasis of Charity

In the desert of need, we all take a sip,
A double shot of kindness, let it not slip.
With a wink and a giggle, we pass it around,
Turning frowns into smiles, it's the best we've found.

Like cactus in bloom, we spread laughter wide,
A quirky dance party, let our joy be our guide.
With sandwiches flying, and jokes in the air,
We feast on goodwill, friendship's delicious fare.

Chronicles of Kind Acts

Once a squirrel stole a nut from a pie,
Panic erupted! Oh my, oh my!
But a wise owl said with a grin so wide,
'Let's bake another, we have love as our guide!'

The town threw a party, with snacks stuffed galore,
Squirrels and owls danced, laughter in store.
With every share, the pie became more,
Parties get wild when we open the door!

A Gratitude Labyrinth

In a maze of thank-yous, we do a quick twist,
Getting lost in a smile, how could we resist?
With each corner we turn, a dance step we take,
Grateful for the laughter, no need for a break.

Balloons flying high, in gratitude's flair,
One says, 'I owe you,' while tossing my hair.
We laugh at the chaos, embracing the fun,
A labyrinth of glee, under the warm sun!

The Glow of Thoughtful Generosity

At the market of nice, we trade a kind word,
For a hug and a smile that's rarely deferred.
An old man offers gum, sweet as can be,
While a kid with a cookie says, 'Share it with me!'

The glow of our hearts, shining ever so bright,
Turns mundane into magic, a beautiful sight.
With kindness in pockets and laughter on keys,
We jam with the world, making music with ease.

Embracing the Offering

A gift of socks, oh what a sight,
In neon colors, shining bright.
I gave you sweets, you gave me a shoe,
Let's trade our laughter, that'll do too!

With late-night snacks and jokes galore,
We share our treasures, who could want more?
A pizza slice, a cup of tea,
Your smile's the best gift, don't you see?

Synergy of Souls

Two heads are better, or so they say,
Especially when we both misplay.
I brought the straws, you brought the fun,
Together we shine like the summer sun.

Your karaoke skills hit a high note,
While I just shout without a coat.
In this odd mix, joy's the prize,
Our silly antics are the best ties.

The Dance of Altruism

Let's share our clumsiness on the floor,
You trip, I laugh; let's dance some more.
We'll twirl and giggle, the world might spin,
In this wild waltz, we both must win!

A sandwich swap? What a delight,
You munch my pickles, what a sight!
In every stumble, we find our grace,
Life's a party; let's embrace!

Radiance in Reciprocity

You baked a cake, I found a cat,
I'd trade both for a tip of your hat.
In pie and purrs, friendship flows,
Each moment shared, our laughter grows.

I'll gift you jokes, you'll share the fries,
In silly exchanges, joy always lies.
From treasure hunts to pillow fights,
Our bond is bright, like city lights!

Tides of Giving

A sandwich shared with grinning glee,
With chips that crunch, a jubilee.
When friends just laugh and tales take flight,
Even stale bread feels just right.

A cat that steals your favorite chair,
But shares a purr, it's only fair.
With every scratch, a dance of paws,
Who knew love had such sharp claws?

A garden grown from scraps and seeds,
Beetle battles, daring deeds.
While weeds might wage an endless fight,
We giggle, best friends, through the night.

Embraces of Benevolence

A hug that's tight, yet arms so wide,
A perfect squeeze, no place to hide.
With laughter bouncing, spirits rise,
Each jest a gift beneath the skies.

A cookie jar that's far too small,
With crumbs and crumbs—there's love for all!
A cookie thief that leaves no trace,
As hugs then blossom in their place.

The chair you let your pal sit in,
Gives room for love, and cheeky grins.
We play our parts in this parade,
All for the joy that's sweetly made.

The Lightness of Gifts Given

A bright balloon that's lost in air,
Drifting here, then floating there.
With giggles shared beneath the sun,
Each gift a joke, a playful pun.

An old sweater, cozy and bright,
Worn inside out, that feels just right.
With mismatched socks, we dance around,
In silly joy, our hearts are crowned.

A quirky hat that shows your flair,
With feathers plumed, you're quite the pair!
When laughter bounces off the walls,
Each moment shared, a love that calls.

Unseen Blessings

A hidden note beneath your plate,
With doodles drawn, it's never late.
Each morning brings a sneaky grin,
As joy appears where spills begin.

A friend who shares their mismatched socks,
In laughter's grip, we beat the clocks.
With silly tales and pranks galore,
Those unseen gifts leave us wanting more.

The luck of finding one lost shoe,
That pairs up well with friends so true.
In every quirk, we find the bliss,
Embraces wrapped in joy's sweet kiss.

The Warmth of Giving Souls

In a world of socks mismatched,
One gave a pair, the other hatched.
They laughed and danced like kids at play,
Grateful hearts brightened the day.

With cookies baked and pies laid bare,
They shared a slice, with utmost care.
A joke about a cat with shoes,
And laughter flowed, their spirits grew.

Each high-five sent kindness around,
Like confetti tossed upon the ground.
Their generosity, a wild spree,
Where giggles echoed, wild and free.

So cheers to those who like to share,
Who find joy in the simple fare.
In silly acts, their hearts align,
Building warmth, like toast and brine.

Unfolding Generosity

A man with hats stacked way too high,
Decided to let one slip by.
He tossed a cap like it was fun,
And shouted, "Now we all have one!"

A woman gave her sweater bold,
To keep a chilly dog from cold.
They laughed, her dog, a sight to see,
With fashion sense, as fine as thee.

They wrapped up gifts in bright, wild paper,
Pretended each was a saber taper.
With every roll, they shouted "Hooray!"
Who knew that fun could stand this way?

So in this dance of give and take,
With laughter sprouting everywhere we wake,
We find the joy in simple deeds,
And plant the laughter, like garden seeds.

Whispered Thanks

A whisper shared beneath the moon,
A pie was baked, they'd sing a tune.
With each sweet slice, they'd let out glee,
Gratitude served up with a spree.

One brought a dance, the other a jest,
They turned the night into a fest.
Thanks sent flying like paper planes,
In their world, joy simply reigns.

Through chuckles and snickers they exchanged,
Each gift unwrapped, delight arranged.
A silly hat upon a head,
Had everyone giggling instead.

So let's raise a toast, a funny cheer,
To all the souls who bring us near.
In whispered thanks, their hearts do dance,
In the rhythm of fun, they take their chance.

Echoing Generosity

A puppet show of gifts galore,
One danced, while others hit the floor.
With silly antics, they did delight,
Making kindness soar like a kite.

They shared bananas, chipped away,
At humor's edge, they'd laugh and play.
"Who needs a peeling?" one did say,
As laughter rang like bells in May.

A heart so big, it could not fit,
Inside a room, not even a bit.
With hugs that felt like giant bears,
They multiplied their love in pairs.

On this day of fun's parade,
The spirit of sharing was displayed.
Echoes of laughter, joy entwined,
A treasure found by hearts so kind.

Hands Open Wide

With pockets empty, still I share,
A half-eaten sandwich, if you dare!
Laughter spills from lips so wide,
As crumbs of kindness stem the tide.

My dog joins in, with drooling glee,
He thinks my gifts are meant for he!
A wagging tail and goofy grin,
Makes generosity a win-win.

We toss our change like candy treats,
To strangers on the crowded streets.
With every coin, a jest or pun,
Leaving behind a trail of fun.

So raise your hands, don't be afraid,
Let joy and laughter be displayed!
For in this dance, the world we cheer,
With open hearts and charm sincere.

The Symphony of Shared Blessings

A clumsy band plays out of tune,
With pots and pans, we'll make our swoon!
Each clang and clash's a silly jest,
As kindness shines, we're truly blessed.

The trombone's stuck, the violin's screech,
But smiles and giggles are within reach.
A tambourine tossed can start a dream,
Where laughter's flowing like a stream.

We share the stage, some silly moves,
Dancing in shoes that have no grooves!
Each awkward twirl, a gift of cheer,
In this wacky concerto, we persevere.

So play along, come join the fun,
Every note shared is never done!
In this grand symphony, we find our place,
With crooked smiles, let's embrace.

Unveiling the Golden Heart

A treasure chest that's filled with jokes,
With each one shared, a laugh provokes.
Lift the lid, find giggles galore,
For giving's what we all adore!

A cookie here, a brownie there,
I bake with love, but crumbs I spare.
"Who took the last bite?" I ask with glee,
"Was it you or that sneaky bee?"

So gather 'round, let stories flow,
Of silly times and mishaps that glow.
With open hearts, we'll share our tales,
As golden laughter never fails.

Unveil that heart, let kindness bloom,
In this hilarious, joyful room!
For in each chuckle and each smart quip,
We find a bond that none can rip.

Winds of Thankfulness

A gust of cheer blows through the town,
Where smiles outshine the saddest frown.
With windy play and quirky prance,
We give and share, a merry dance.

Forget me nots on every breeze,
A windy day makes wishes tease.
We toss our thanks like autumn leaves,
In swirling laughter, everyone believes!

An umbrella flips, a hat takes flight,
In this light-hearted, breezy night.
Thankfulness swirls in funny ways,
As we share joy on windy days.

So let the winds of kindness blow,
In every laugh, let love overflow!
As we ride the breeze, hand in hand,
Together we create our own land.

Ripples of Kindred Spirits

A squirrel shared a nut with me,
I thought it was quite the spree.
He chattered in playful delight,
I offered him a cookie in bright.

The dog next door sniffed my shoe,
He wagged his tail, what else to do?
I tossed him a ball, he raced with glee,
While I wondered, was it him or me?

A neighbor knocked, all covered in mud,
He brought a pie, his face like a bud.
I laughed too hard, it fell on the floor,
He slipped, then asked for a bit more.

In this town, we trade smiles galore,
A gift, a laugh, and maybe more.
With each tiny act of cheer,
The world gets brighter, that much is clear.

The Symphony of Altruism

A chicken crossed the road to dance,
Gave me a wink, took a chance.
I laughed so loud, the cows looked on,
With horns held high, they joined the con!

A cat with a bowtie played the flute,
While mice in tuxedos sang, oh so cute.
I tossed them some cheese, they twirled with glee,
A musical party, wild and free!

The sun peeked in, took a bow,
As flowers giggled, 'Oh wow!'
Gratitude sparkled in the air,
While bees brought honey, oh what a fair!

We cheered together, hearts in tune,
Under the watch of a laughing moon.
A symphony of fun to be,
Notes of kindness, the best harmony.

Bridges Built on Thanks

A paper boat floated on by,
With a thank you note set to fly.
I waved at it, it waved back too,
A bridge of cheer, who knew it could do?

A cat on my porch, eyeing my treats,
Gave a little purr; oh, what sweet feats!
I shared a snack, he rolled in delight,
We built a bridge, side by side, alright!

A grumpy old man brought me a pie,
Said, 'It's my recipe, give it a try!'
I offered a smile, he laughed at the fate,
'Thanks for the sugar; this could be great!'

Together we learned, laughs all around,
Building bridges from joy we found.
With silly gestures, we'd never part,
United in kindness, a masterful art.

In the Garden of Warmth

In the garden where daisies grow,
A rabbit hopped in a fancy bow.
I offered him carrots, fresh from the plot,
He danced in circles, giving a snot!

A ladybug waltzed on a leaf,
Sharing her secrets, a comedic chief.
With every laugh, the flowers bloomed,
The trees sighed softly, happiness zoomed!

The sun played peek-a-boo with the sky,
While worms hosted races, oh, my oh my!
I cheered for the winners, threw up some seeds,
A garden of joy, fulfilled all our needs.

In our garden of warmth and cheer,
Every visitor spread lasting good cheer.
With quirks and giggles, we all took part,
Creating a masterpiece, all from the heart.

The Embrace of Giving Souls

A cat gave a dog a new ball,
Said, "Fetch it if you can, after all!"
The dog barked back with a chuckle,
"I'd rather you just bring me a Snuffle!"

A friend brought lunch from the fridge,
His sandwich was huge—a whole smidge!
"I'll trade you so much for a crumb,"
He said, "Come on, don't be so glum!"

They laughed and swapped bites, what a scene,
Who knew old bread could taste so keen?
And gratitude danced on the table,
As they filled their bellies, feeling quite stable!

In the end, it's the joy that we spread,
With laughter and snacks, there's plenty ahead!
Life's moments are meant to be shared,
With a wink and a grin, feel the love declared!

A Canvas of Merry Altruism

A painter gave colors to a black sheep,
"This isn't just wool, it's art!" he did leap.
The sheep looked down, feeling so bright,
"I'd love to be famous, oh what a sight!"

A baker once shared his flour stash,
"With icing on top, let's make a smash!"
They decorated cakes in the yard,
A sugar rush left them both quite jarred!

They laughed at the mess, icing on their nose,
"Let's make this a party, who would oppose?"
With sprinkles and giggles, they painted the sky,
In the world of giving, they aimed to fly!

In a painted scene of vibrant glee,
Generosity echoed through the jubilee.
Each stroke, a story, a shared delight,
Merry hearts dance, thankful all night!

Winds of Generous Intent

A squirrel threw acorns to a bear,
"Here you go, buddy, I don't really care!"
The bear caught one and took a taste,
"These are crunchy, no need to waste!"

A bird chirped along with a jolly tune,
"Perhaps I'll share a seed or two soon!"
The skies were filled with cheerful cries,
As laughter spread wider than blue skies!

Fills of joy in the forest air,
Every creature found their flair!
Squirrels danced, and the bear sang loud,
Creating a giving, merry crowd!

With every acorn and every song,
In this wild world, they all belong.
Winds of intent spun high and free,
A tapestry of fun, just let it be!

The Mosaic of Empathy

A clumsy friend tripped on his shoelace,
Brought laughter and giggles to the whole place.
"I meant to do that!" he grinned so wide,
And soon everyone joined him for a ride!

A neighbor shared muffins, a whimsical treat,
"One bite is sweet, let's make it a feat!"
Everyone gathered for crumbs and a laugh,
Gleeful together, a joyful craft!

They painted the town with smiles galore,
In every corner, generosity swore.
With muffins in hand and hearts full of fun,
An awkward stumble brought everyone to run!

So here we stand, in a mosaic bright,
With humor and kindness, we spin delight.
Each piece fits perfectly, oh what a show,
Together in laughter, the spirits do glow!

The Dance of Giving

In a world so bright and airy,
A pig waltzes, oh so merry!
He twirls and flings his golden coins,
While dodging cows with silly groins.

The moonbeam laughs, a chuckle loud,
As chickens join this quirky crowd.
They flap their wings, the gifts they fling,
A jig of joy, oh what a swing!

A cat in boots, with swag and tease,
Shares snacks with birds, they munch with ease.
They dance on rooftops, full of cheer,
With every step, they spread good cheer!

Now here's the twist in this grand spree,
The mouse near cheese shouts, "Dance with me!"
They hop and bop, both small and tall,
With laughter echoing, one and all.

Threads of Benevolence

A spider spins with great delight,
A web of care, oh what a sight!
She offers flies a cozy spot,
But, oh, the flies, they just don't plot!

The squirrel hops with acorn stash,
He shares his nuts with quite a splash.
But all the while, he's on the run,
From raucous friends who want some fun!

An owl dozes, wise and old,
While hedgehogs trade their quirks of gold.
One pricks a toe, it's all in jest,
"Let's share our troubles, it's for the best!"

In this land of playful glee,
They weave their fate, just wait and see.
For kindness comes with laughter sweet,
Creating bonds that are hard to beat!

Whispers of Hearts Uniting

A turtle whispers to a hare,
"Let's share our dreams without a care!"
The hare, confused, says with a grin,
"Are you sure we won't just spin?"

A porcupine offers hugs so tight,
But owls hoot, "That's not quite right!"
They bob and weave, a friendly game,
One tiny prick, fair hearts not lame!

A llama prances, bold and loud,
"Let's have a dance, come join the crowd!"
With every step, the hearts align,
Together weaving tales divine.

So let's unite in quirks untold,
With laughter shared, our spirits bold.
In whispers soft, we find our way,
Creating joy in every play!

Seeds of Appreciation

A farmer plants with hopeful grin,
Seeds of kindness scattered thin.
But wait! A goat eats every sprout,
While chuckling loud, "What's this about?"

The sun shines bright, the rain falls light,
And plants grow tall, oh what a sight!
Yet every time they dost take root,
A band of mice slips in to loot!

With every bite, they squeak with glee,
"More soon to come, oh joy, you'll see!"
This silly game of give and take,
Brings laughs and crumbs, a joyful make!

So here we gather, seeds in hand,
Sharing laughter, oh isn't it grand?
In this garden of give and send,
We find the love that never ends!

The Generosity in the Little Things

A cookie shared is a smile given,
It's free and sweet, like a joy-driven mitten.
An extra fry from my plate to yours,
Who knew love could come in fast food stores?

A hug that's tight, like a bear in a cram,
Can change a day, make sadness go slam!
So let's spread kindness in layers like cake,
With sprinkles of laughter that no one can fake.

Seedlings of Hope

I planted a seed, thought it a gift,
Turns out it's a weed, oh such a rift!
But I watered with care, watched it grow tall,
And laughed when it bloomed, all over the wall.

In life's little garden, we reap and we sow,
With thank-you notes tangled in sweet row after row.
To neighbors, like gnomes, let's all take a chance,
And dance with our weeds in a generous prance.

A Legacy of Caring

Remember the time we shared that last pie?
You took half, I took none, oh my!
But the laughter we shared was more than the crust,
In this odd little tale, it's the love we trust.

Wrap your kindness in bubble wrap bright,
Let's bounce together, it's a joyful flight!
For each hug that we give, there's a giggle in store,
When you share your heart, there's always room for more.

Touchstones of Thankfulness

A compliment's a rainbow, free to give,
"And your hair looks nice!" makes anyone live.
It's the little things that lift us up high,
Like finding a dollar, oh my, oh my!

So toss in some humor with every "thank you,"
A wink and a nod, like we're one big crew.
When we spread cheer, like confetti on cake,
The best kind of giving is fun that we make.

Love's Abiding Influence

In a garden where kindness grows,
You'll find laughter hiding in the rows.
Gardener gurgles as he sows a seed,
While his buddy chases an errant weed.

A lovebird swoops, with style it flaunts,
Wings flapping wildly, it hilariously taunts.
Neighbors giggle, sharing tales of cheer,
As they swap homemade pies and a pint of beer.

Barking dogs join the joyful din,
Chasing shadows, where mischief begins.
A cat leaps high, with a cotton fluff tail,
As love scampers forth, leaving hearts in its trail.

So let's dance in this merriment made,
And throw confetti where hearts are displayed.
For in each chuckle, a bond will ignite,
And love's abiding influence sparkles so bright.

Chasing the Light of Compassion

A puppy prances, wearing its bow,
Chasing after kindness, do you know?
With a wagging tail and a goofy grin,
It tries to catch laughter—small things win.

A squirrel stashes snacks with flair,
While a generous friend steals a chair.
Their antics blend like peanut and jelly,
Squirrels and friends, what a funny medley!

In the park, with sunshine galore,
A kid slips on grass, and they all roar.
For every tumble, there's kindness to spare,
Compassion shines brightly in the fresh air.

So let's race each other, hand in hand,
With giggles and joy, oh isn't it grand?
Chasing the light means we trip and discover,
That laughter's the thread linking us all like a cover.

The Bridge of Open Hands

There's a bridge made of hearts and feasts,
Where everyone gathers, from the West to the East.
A pie rolls off, and oh what a sight,
As hands burst open in hilarious delight!

With open arms, a potluck amass,
Bringing quirks in mismatched glass.
A jello creation that wiggles with cheer,
Starts a dance party; do you want to join here?

Fried chicken plops and the crowd squeals,
While dad cracks a joke, and laughter reveals.
A toast is made with lemonade glasses,
Clinking together, they celebrate masses!

So cross this bridge, don't be shy,
With open hands, let the spirit fly.
For in this marvellous, silly stance,
Generosity leads us all to dance!

The Embrace of Generous Spirits

In a forest of giggles, the trees stand tall,
Where squirrels share acorns and prompts to install.
A bear in a bow tie, what a sight to see,
Offering honey in cups, as sweet as can be.

Feathers float down from a comical bird,
As we laugh at the antics; haven't you heard?
The great hawk overhead provides sage advice,
"Act kind and generous, it's the best slice of life."

At each friendly hug, a tickle arrives,
And laughter erupts as surprise high-fives.
So let's share our treasures, big or quite small,
With generous spirits, who giggle and call.

In this humorous haven, the heart warmly beams,
Where kindness abounds and everyone dreams.
Join the embrace of this joyous affair,
And wear your best laughter, if you dare!

The Sunshine of Thus Far

Thank you for the sun so bright,
But did you feed my cat last night?
With every laugh, a gift you share,
Just don't ask me to repair my hair!

Your hugs are warm, a sweet delight,
Like coffee served with extra fright.
It's funny how you say you care,
But I still want a better chair!

With silly jokes and playful cheer,
You make the tough days disappear.
So here's my toast, a bit absurd,
To you, my friend, the funniest bird!

Let's raise a glass, let's spill some tea,
I'll give you laughs; you give me glee.
Together we'll create a scene,
Of joyful moments, pure and clean!

Unwritten Kindness

Your kindness is a hidden gem,
Like finding socks without the hem.
The way you smile, it lights the room,
But where's the cake? That's my next zoom!

You offer help with style and flair,
But I still think you'll steal my chair.
With all your quirks and silly ways,
You make my dullest nights a blaze!

Like bubbles bursting in the air,
Your laughter floats without a care.
We'll dance the jig, we'll make it wild,
Just know, my friend, you're still a child!

If kindness had a price to pay,
You'd find a way to give it away.
But hey, my friend, don't worry much,
I'll keep your heart, it's gold, my crutch!

The Treasure of Selfless Giving

You say your treasure is your heart,
But do you have a shopping cart?
You give so much, it's quite absurd,
Last week you tripped on your own word!

Your laughter rings, a priceless sound,
Like pants that fit but never found.
With every deed, you steal the show,
Just make sure you don't trip like so!

A gift of joy you freely share,
Your curious cats are quite a pair.
With every hug, I feel the glee,
Just don't expect much from my tea!

So here's a cheer for all you do,
With humor bright and kindness true.
Let's feast on fries, let's share a laugh,
In this great tale, we're both the half!

A Garden of Goodwill

In the garden of our shared delight,
You plant the seeds of joy each night.
With puns that make the flowers giggle,
You sprout a smile, it's quite the wiggle!

Your generosity's a clown on the run,
Turning mundane days into pure fun.
You sprinkle kindness like confetti,
Just please don't bring your pet yeti!

We reap what we sow, that's a fact,
Your goofy spirit's our perfect act.
As weeds of worry fade away,
Let's dance and laugh, just like ballet!

So here's to blooms and sunny skies,
To all the laughter with no goodbyes.
A garden full of love and cheer,
With you around, I have no fear!

Bridges of Benevolence

In a town where cookies flowed,
The baker gave them to a toad.
The frog, quite clever, took a stack,
Then hopped away with a silly quack.

A dog ran by with pizza flair,
Snatching slices from the air.
The people laughed, oh what a sight,
As dinner turned into a froggy flight!

Neighbors shared their quirky woes,
Like giving hugs to a bunch of crows.
With every giggle, they found a way,
To spread their joy on a sunny day!

So raise your glasses, don't be shy,
For bridges bloom when we just try.
With laughter shared, our hearts align,
In quirky acts, we shall entwine.

Abundance in the Simple

A cat named Lenny wore a hat,
He thought it made him look so fat.
But when he danced, oh what a sight,
The mice all cheered with pure delight.

A spoon was lost, but found a friend,
In a bowl of soup, its cozy end.
They stirred each other with delight,
Creating flavors day and night.

The neighbors shared their strange attire,
Old socks and hats, a jester's choir.
With every mix of wacky wear,
They laughed until they spilled their fare!

So here's to joy, in small and grand,
From silly acts, we'll take a stand.
In every laugh, abundance grows,
Through all the quirks that life bestows.

The Canvas of Generosity

A painter once used jelly beans,
To craft a world of candy scenes.
With every swoosh of vibrant hue,
He'd share his sweets, to hearts so true.

A monkey stole a brush one day,
And painted stripes in bold array.
With splashes here and splatters there,
The jungle danced; who needs a chair?

The sun beamed down on pinstripe skies,
As giggles echoed, oh so wise.
An art fair formed, with laughs to share,
While lemonade dreams floated in air.

So paint your world with kindness bright,
In every stroke, find pure delight.
For laughter colors all we do,
In this canvas, come join the crew.

Seeds of Thankfulness

A squirrel named Gus had acorns galore,
He offered some snacks to a hungry boar.
The pig squealed joyfully as he munched,
Turns out friendship starts with a lunch!

A wise old owl gave some hugs away,
To the rabbits who danced in the sun all day.
With every gesture, big or small,
They found their way to brighten all.

The flowers laughed, swaying in glee,
As bees buzzed 'round—a busy spree!
They shared their pollen and sweet delight,
Each thank-you song a joyful flight.

So here's to sharing all our cheer,
From acorns to hugs, let's persevere.
For seeds of kindness bring forth our best,
In laughter's harvest, we are truly blessed.

Threads of Generosity

A neighbor dropped by with cookies in hand,
I thought, 'What a deal! It's a sweet little band.'
Then I saw the sprinkles, a rainbow delight,
    I figured that sharing was only polite.

My cat eyed the treats, with a glint in her gaze,
I handed her one, but she turned it ablaze.
We laughed at the mess, what a hilarious sight,
    For generosity's chaos can be quite a bite.

A friend gave a plant, said 'Don't let it die!'
But it looked at me like it was meant to fly.
With watering can in hand, I did all of that,
Now it's thriving while wearing a cute little hat.

So let's raise a toast to odd gifts we share,
Each quirky exchange brings a comic flair.
For laughter and kindness go hand in hand,
    And together they dance, like a zany band.

A Tapestry of Thanks

I crafted a gift for my friend down the street,
Wrapped it in socks—that was quite the treat!
She opened it laughing, and squealed with delight,
Who knew laundry socks could be such a sight?

We laughed as she tried to wear one on her head,
'Fashion statement!' she said, 'Now I'll never dread!'
So off to the grocery store, we pranced and we peeked,
With nutty sock hats, we really looked chic.

A pie made of veggies went flying like that,
'Then my cat grabbed a slice. Is he really that fat?'
We snickered and giggled at the mess on the floor,
The joys of thanks spark laughter galore.

So in this wild quilt of vibrant mishaps,
Each thread tells a story, with punchlines and claps.
Together we weave a bright, happy stash,
In the tapestry of life, let's giggle and clash.

The Art of Giving Freely

I bought a big cake and forgot all the forks,
So we dug in with fingers, oh, what fun, folks!
A scoop and a smear, with frosting galore,
We danced around crumbs, making quite the score.

Then someone brought fruit with a twist of pun,
Wielding a banana like it was a gun.
Our laughter erupted, sugar filled the air,
Life's little follies create chaos to share.

An old sofa found home with a cheerful new pair,
Who bounced on the springs without any care.
'This treasure's got style, we'll call it our throne!'
As the cushions flew off, I thought, 'We've grown.'

Generosity's art can be utterly nuts,
From cakes to the couches, absurdity cuts.
But oh what a joy when we freely engage,
In laughter-filled moments—our own silly stage.

Ripples of Goodwill

A dollar for coffee turned into a spree,
Each sip of that latte, tasted like glee.
I paid for the stranger, who winked at the sun,
Now we're both caffeinated, ready for fun.

A cat at the café squawked 'I'll lend you my charm,'
'Your kindness in pastries has me feeling warm.'
So we shared some croissants while pretending to sing,
The ripples of goodwill made our hearts take wing.

I dropped off some donuts at work for my mates,
But they vanished like magic, oh, don't tempt the fates!
'Let us bring donuts next week,' they all chimed,
With promises floating—sweet treats we'll find.

So here's to the joy in the silly and bright,
To ripples of kindness that spark pure delight.
From lattes to laughter, we twirl and we sway,
In the dance of goodwill, let's play all day!

Notes of Thankful Hearts

Scribbles on napkins, big thanks out loud,
For the coffee spills shared, we're grateful and proud.
Each crumpled note whispers, 'You're the best!'
Even if you stole fries, at my lunch, no jest!

A gift card to nowhere, what a delight,
With a mug that says, 'I'm worth a bite.'
Your bouquet of coupons, makes my day bright,
In this game of kindness, let's take flight!

So here's to the giggles, the laughter inside,
For the times you picked me, on that crazy ride.
For the hugs that you give, and the smiles we find,
In this wacky circus, our hearts intertwined.

With a sparkle of mischief, and a dash of grace,
Thankful hearts meeting, in this glorious space.
Let's raise our cups high, to the joy we impart,
In the dance of our lives, gratitude's the art.

Bell Tolls of Benevolence

Ring-a-ling, the bell chimes, what a sound!
For the kindness we share, it knows no bound.
A donut for your troubles, here's one for me,
Because life's too short to sip tea bitterly.

Swapping baked goods like trading cards,
You brought me cookies, I brought you lards.
The calorie counts? Let's just ignore,
We're fueling joy, that's what friends are for!

With laughter that echoes, and stories that spread,
A slap on the back, to lighten the dread.
In this town of gestures, both big and small,
What's a little goodness, if shared by all?

So when the bell tolls, don't just stand still,
Join the joyful noise, feel the festive thrill.
With a wink and a nudge, let's spread the cheer,
In the symphony of kindness, come lend your ear.

A Kindness Danced

Two left feet on the floor, but we'll try,
With kindness as our rhythm, let's reach for the sky.
A jiggle of joy, we're stepping along,
In this dance of giving, can't get it wrong!

So here's my arm, let's twirl and twist,
With every silly move, joy can't be missed.
The laughter that bubbles, like a fizzy drink,
In the chaos of care, we'll never sink!

With each generous beat, our spirits grow,
Yours is the tune, wear it like a bow.
No shoes required, just follow your heart,
In this waltz of kindness, we'll never part.

So let's dance together, through thick and thin,
With hugs like confetti, let the fun begin!
As the music plays on, let our laughter enhance,
In this carnival of love, we'll forever dance!

The Gift of Togetherness

Popcorn in hand, we're ready, it's true,
To binge on old sitcoms, just me and you.
With shared giggles and snacks, we'll laugh till we cry,
Who knew that growing old would make us fly?

Unpacking the memories, like gifts in a box,
The jokes we traded, no need for a fox.
From turkey dinners to weather banter,
Every moment shared makes the heart feel lighter.

The cozy chaos, like socks that don't mate,
Trust me, that mismatch is our special fate.
Like ketchup on fries, we fit hand in glove,
In this circus of life, we're made for love!

So here's to the moments, both silly and grand,
To laughter and joy, as we go hand in hand.
In the gift of togetherness, we'll forever stay,
Bouncing through life, like kids in a play!

A Tidal Wave of Thankfulness

Waves crash with smiles so wide,
Thanks float in on ebbing tide.
I trip over gratitude's feet,
As gratitude swaggered down the street.

I spilled my thanks like a cup gone wrong,
My neighbor laughed, 'You've got it strong!'
Dancing forks and wobbly spoons,
Thankful tunes beneath the moon.

The sea of thanks roars and swells,
Even my cat can tell it smells.
Fish with hats swim by with flair,
While I wave my hands in midair.

Thankfulness wears a silly grin,
Juggling pies with a belly spin.
Surfers, they ride the wave, oh gee!
"Can you catch some for me?" they plea.

Kindness in Motion

Kindness rolled in, what a sight,
Scooting on a bike with delight.
Handing out hugs like candy bars,
"Get yours quick! They won't last far!"

A chicken crossed just to say thanks,
Leaving behind its goofy pranks.
I offered some buttered toast,
Now it's the town's feathered host!

A busker strums with love in his tune,
While squirrels dance beneath the moon.
"Tip your hat!" a lady shouted loud,
Kindness is truly its own proud crowd.

As laughter pops like bubble gum,
We spread kindness, oh so glum!
Riding the breeze with a goofy cheer,
Come join us, the kind crew is here!

The Heart's Overflowing Cup

My heart's a cup, spilling over tea,
With muffins that giggle and scones that flee.
Pouring love, it's quite a sight,
Pastries plotting a playful flight!

Friends arrive with giddy grins,
Taking sips while chaos begins.
One trips, a cookie flies high,
Hitting the ceiling, oh my, oh my!

We toast with juice to the skies,
Swelling hearts, we'll share our fries.
Laughter echoes, never ends,
All this joy from silly friends.

The cup may spill but never break,
With rocky roads and a huge cheesecake.
Together we'll fill the world with cheer,
In this cup of smiles, you're always near!

A Symphony of Shared Joy

Join the band of silly notes,
As gratitude giggles in our throats.
A tuba's honk meets a flute's sweet trills,
Making music with all our skills.

We march in socks that don't quite match,
Each step a dance, a joyful scratch.
With tambourines made of empty jars,
We tap to the rhythm of neighborly cars.

Joy spills over, splashes in between,
A symphony of laughter, so keen.
Riding waves of a whipped cream sound,
Our hearts in concert, joyfully bound.

So raise your spoons and forks high,
Let's serenade the fluffy sky.
In our shared joy, let's play along,
Together we sing our silly song!

The Light of Selfless Acts

In a cafe, I paid for my friend,
He laughed so hard, said, "You're my godsend!"
The bill was huge, I tried to hide,
But in generosity, I took it in stride.

A cat on the street, I gave it my fries,
It looked at me funny, with big, round eyes.
I told it a joke, it seemed to grin,
Turns out, furballs are the best kind of kin.

Helped an old lady, crossing the way,
She handed me cookies—what a sweet pay!
I thought I was the hero, oh my dear,
But she had the secret, I volunteer here!

So here's to the laughs from kindness we spread,
Like wearing mismatched socks on our head.
Let's dance in the joy of giving a hand,
And make the world smile, isn't it grand?

Blossoms of Appreciation

A flower for you, it's not what it seems,
It's plastic! But hey, your smile redeems.
We giggled together, like kids in a park,
Sharing odd treasures, it's quite a lark.

Compliments flung like confetti in air,
"Your hair's like a cloud," I teased with a flare.
You tossed a banana, and I dove to defend,
Generosity's tricky, especially with friends.

Baked you a cake, but forgot all the yeast,
A flat little pancake emerged, to say the least.
You cheered like a champion, "Best thing I've had!"
Together we danced, feeling silly but glad.

Grateful for moments, absurd but so real,
Spreading good vibes is the ultimate meal.
Let's plant some humor, watch laughter grow,
In a garden of joy, let our kindness flow.

The Circle of Kind Deeds

Tossed a penny, wishing for good,
But got soaked instead, misunderstood.
A splash from a puddle, laughter did spread,
Generous chaos, filling our head.

I helped my mate move—what a disaster!
He lost my pizza with speed—now that's faster!
Yet through all the boxes and lost furry pets,
We claimed it a victory—no regrets yet.

Trading my sandwich for chips and some juice,
You never know what deal you might choose.
We laughed till we cried at the flavors we shared,
Bonkers and bold, like two clowns unprepared.

So join in the fun, let's keep up the pace,
Generosity's dance is a joyous embrace.
With giggles and chuckles, let's form our own creed,
In a circle of kindness, we all plant a seed.

Illuminating Lives

I borrowed your pen, but lost it, oh dear!
You tossed me a grin, "It's okay, never fear."
We laughed about ink stains all over the sheets,
Your kind heart shines bright, it never retreats.

A lunch for a friend sometimes turns to a feast,
But you made me giggle, said, "I'll bring the yeast!"
Homemade bread flopped, like a flop in a show,
Yet we chewed through the laughter, on we did go.

Sweet little favors, a cup for your tea,
You spilled it on me, "Guess that one's for free!"
We wiped it off together, two clowns in a play,
In our mismatched socks, we celebrate each day.

So here's to the moments, the silly and small,
In lighting the world, we can all have a ball.
With kindness as our beacon, let's tackle the stride,
Together, with laughter, there's nowhere to hide.

Echoes of Kindness

A cat brought me a shoe today,
It wasn't mine, but hey, that's okay.
The dog was jealous, barked quite loud,
Both proud and silly, a mismatched crowd.

A squirrel knocked on my window sharp,
Demanding acorns, like a pop star's harp.
I tossed him one, with a wink and a grin,
He danced on the ledge, let the fun begin!

Neighbors came over for a potluck feast,
I burned the bread, they ate it at least!
Laughter erupted, spilled on the floor,
This kitchen chaos, who could want more?

A bouquet of flowers, from a friend so dear,
Turned into a hat, oh my, what a cheer!
We twirled in circles, wearing floral crowns,
In this silly dance, never wore frowns.

The Heart's Abundant Exchange

I baked a cake, but forgot the sugar,
It turned out salty, a taste like a booger!
My friends laughed hard, what a hilarious sight,
They still ate it up, they must've been polite!

A generous friend brought me some pies,
One had a filling that made grown men cry.
We laughed till we snorted, our faces went red,
In this feast of joy, nothing was said.

I gifted my pal a shiny old spoon,
She thought it was gold, let out a loud swoon.
We dug through junk, found treasures galore,
In this quirky exchange, we always want more!

With giggles and gifts taped up with some flair,
We wrapped up our hearts, tossed laughter in air.
In this dance of kindness, what a wild spree,
You bring some giggles, I'll bring the glee!

Harvest of Thankfulness

I picked some tomatoes, thought they looked grand,
But they splat on the floor, what a sticky land!
We all giggled, made salsa instead,
Dancing in circles, avoiding the spread.

A pie on the table, but oh, not for me,
The dog had his turn, oh, what a sight to see!
With crumbs on his nose, he gave me a wink,
Our shared gratitude, a moment to think.

We sat 'round the fire, swapped stories of yore,
About a lost sock or a cat by the door.
Every tale ending with laughter that glows,
The warmth of our friendship, it just overflows.

A basket of goodies, we tossed up high,
It landed on grandma, oh me, oh my!
She laughed so hard, it shook up her cane,
In our harvest of joy, there's always a gain!

Gifts Beyond Measure

I wrapped up a gift, a wild surprise,
But it popped open, what a grand rise!
Confetti exploded, went everywhere,
We laughed so hard, without any care.

A turtle named Turbo came for a race,
He won, but I tripped, fell flat on my face!
The ducks laughed along, quacking their cheer,
In this funny contest, we hold dear.

Homemade cookies, an accidental mix,
Chocolate past the date, oh what a fix!
We munched with glee, though a tad unsure,
In the realm of good snacks, it was quite an allure.

With hearts all full of joy and good fun,
We shared what we had, every last crumb!
In this wild world, the laughter won't cease,
These gifts, these giggles: a true masterpiece!

The Light of Open Hands

In a world so full of cheer,
I dropped my wallet, oh dear!
But a stranger picked it up with glee,
And handed it back—to me!

We laughed about my clumsiness,
He said it's just a messiness.
I offered him a slice of pie,
He grinned and shook his head—oh my!

Next time I'll tie it to my shoes,
To avoid any more blues.
His laughter rolled like waves on sand,
My wallet safe in open hand.

Gratitude for a simple deed,
With a pie, we both agreed:
In life's mishaps, joy we find,
With open hands and hearts combined.

Embracing The Overflow

With coffee cups that spill and slosh,
We share a smile, what a posh!
I said, "Hey there, let's not fret,
I'll share my brew—no need to sweat!"

He took a sip, and then a gulp,
I warned him, "Slow!"—he let out a yelp!
My friend was bouncing off the walls,
From too much coffee, he called for stalls.

In laughter, we created a mess,
Beans everywhere, a coffee dress!
Yet in our chaos, we found the fun,
In overflowing cups, we both were done.

So let us raise our mugs and cheer,
For moments shared, we hold dear.
In spills and thrills, you'll see the glow,
Unity in every coffee flow.

Tides of Compassion

At the beach, I found a crab,
Scuttling by, oh what a blab!
"I'll share my snack," I simply said,
He pinched my finger—time to dread!

We traded chips for salty fries,
He made a face—what a surprise!
With waves around, we laughed out loud,
A crustacean and me—quite the crowd!

Next, I tossed him a candy spree,
He eyed it like, "What's wrong with me?"
He danced away, his joy returned,
In silly moments, my heart had learned.

With laughter echoing in the tide,
In crusty exchanges, we took pride.
A crabby friend and snacks galore,
In kindness shared, we all explore.

Beneath the Canopy of Sharing

Under trees, I threw a picnic,
Food in baskets, quite specific!
But ants arrived—what a delight,
I joined their feast, oh what a sight!

"Please stay away!" I tried to plead,
But they were eager for the feed.
I laughed and shared a crumb or two,
Ants in party hats—who knew?

With my sandwich, I also shared,
My humor—equally bared.
An ant in shades, the lead of show,
Together we brought joy, don't you know?

In nature's arms, we found our place,
In silly acts, we shared our grace.
Beneath the trees, with laughter bright,
Generous hearts in the warm sunlight.

Emblems of Empathy

In a world of snacks and cheer,
One doughnut shared, brings good revere.
A sip of coffee, warm and neat,
We trade our bites, oh what a treat!

A cat that steals your comfy chair,
You let him sit, but man, beware!
He'll purr and nap, and claim that space,
Such empathy in feline grace.

When shoes are tight, and socks are odd,
You trade your pair, and raise a nod.
That mismatched look, a fashion trend,
With gratitude, we all pretend!

So share a laugh, a snack or cheer,
Together we'll conquer, bring good cheer.
Through silly acts, so small and bright,
It's blessings wrapped in pure delight.

Blessings in Action

A friend who bakes with flour galore,
Invites you in, oh what a score!
With cookies warm, and frosting fat,
You nibble, smile, then share the chat.

A plant you forget, it starts to droop,
You gift it joy, with a little hoop.
You paint its pot, make it a shrine,
Together we flourish, so divine!

A game night planned with a quirky twist,
You take some snacks, who could resist?
The dice roll funny, laughter ensues,
With each turn taken, who won't enthuse?

At the end of the day, we find our way,
With full hearts, and laughter at play.
In small acts done with joyous glee,
We build our world, just you and me.

Generous Echoes

A shout of glee, a wink, a nod,
In every gesture, laughter trod.
A birthday wish with cake to share,
We sing it loud, without a care.

A friend in need, with shoes too tight,
Pass those flippers, oh what a sight!
They'll dance and wiggle, but that's just fine,
In generous hearts, we all align.

Some spilled coffee, a silly mess,
We laugh it off, no need to stress.
With paper towels and jokes galore,
We clean it up, then share some more.

So here's the truth, as we all know,
In funny antics, love will grow.
In echoes of joy, we don't grow tired,
With every giggle, our souls are wired.

Weaving Generosity into Life

A puzzle piece that never fits,
You chuckle loud, and share your wits.
You pass it on for others' fun,
Together we laugh, like it's a pun.

A trip to the shop, "Hey, what to buy?"
You take a friend, then wonder why.
They load up carts, with chips and soda,
While giggles rise, it's quite a quota!

In pieces stitched, with laughter's thread,
We build our days, with joy instead.
From silly hats to random pranks,
Each act is gold, it's time for thanks!

So laugh aloud, and don't hold back,
In moments shared, we find our track.
With hearts so light, and spirits bright,
We weave our lives, a true delight.

Resonance of Shared Joy.

In the fridge, leftovers hide,
Cheesy surprise, what a ride!
Sharing lunch, we grin and beam,
Dancing flavors, a foodie dream.

A sock on my head, what a sight!
Caught in a prank, oh what a fright!
Laughter erupts, the room fills with cheer,
In silliness shared, joy's crystal clear.

Old board games tossed, dice at play,
Chasing victory—who's going to sway?
With each roll, we jeer and shout,
In this chaos, love's what it's about.

As we trade our best jokes, side-splitting,
Each punchline hits, we're all acquitting.
In this rhythm, our hearts do attend,
Mirth multiplied, as we share and blend.

Echoes of Kindness

A cat in a hat, a curious sight,
Bringing us laughter, oh what delight!
With whiskers twitching, he steals the show,
In shared giggles, our kindness will grow.

A neighbor's lost pot, so shiny and bright,
Returned with a wink, what a delight!
We trade stories over a cup of tea,
Echoes of kindness, as sweet as can be.

A mishap with cake, it's dropped with a thud,
We laugh as we scoop it out of the mud.
All hands on deck for a dessert redo,
Baking together, our spirits break through.

With socks that don't match, we strut down the street,
Fashion faux pas, but with joy and with heat.
Each mismatched step, a memory spun,
In the echoes of kindness, we all become one.

Hearts in Harmony

On a bike built for two, we wobble and sway,
Pedals against laughter, that's how we play!
With arms around shoulders, we travel in sync,
In friendship's embrace, we laugh till we stink.

A surprise birthday cake with balloons that deflate,
We cheer and we chortle, never too late!
As frosting flies high, our smiles stretch wide,
Heartbeats in laughter, our joys collide.

Spontaneous dances in the living room's glow,
Socks on the tile, we shuffle to and fro.
With each awkward move, more laughter's ignited,
Our hearts beat in rhythm, so joyful, excited!

As we share our dreams, with mismatched attempts,
In the glow of the night, we create happy events.
Hearts in a chorus, singing ballads of cheer,
In silliness found, our love grows ever near.

The Gift of Giving

A rubber chicken may come as a gift,
Yet laughter it brings is an instant uplift.
Toss it around, what a wacky retreat,
In the gift of good humor, we all can compete.

In the garden of jokes, we plant every pun,
Water with laughter, let old grudges run.
With buckets of giggles and shovels of cheer,
The gift of good humor brings everyone near.

A voucher for hugs, come claim your delight,
Wrap up your worries, give laughter a bite!
We barter in smiles, till the sun fancies red,
In this market of joy, we're all widely fed.

The potluck of kindness spreads over the hill,
We feast on the joy, life's bubbling thrill.
As we gather round, with hearts all aglow,
The gift of giving makes relationships grow.

The Rhythm of Care

In a world of give and take,
A pie was baked, but it was fake.
We laughed and shared our silly snack,
Turns out it's all just a little hack.

When we swap our quirks and quirks collide,
One man's treasure is another's glide.
With silly dances, we twirl around,
In this care, our laughs abound.

With wobbly chairs and funky tunes,
We bounced together like cartoon loons.
For every smile, there's a cheeky dance,
We're sprightly kids taking a chance!

So here we are in this frolicsome fray,
Grinning wide through the playful play.
With hearts like balloons ready to soar,
We find the rhythm; we can't help but roar!

Melodies of Mutual Aid

We strum our hearts like a broken guitar,
Each note's a giggle, we're never far.
With quirky tunes and offbeat sighs,
We harmonize through our joyful cries.

Dancing along life's lumpy road,
We share our snacks; I'll share my code.
Come join the fun at our comedy fair,
For every punchline, see the love we wear!

From lopsided mugs to laughter so free,
We sing our songs like a raucous spree.
With words that bounce and hearts that fly,
We build up bridges, oh my oh my!

In this wacky fusion of glad haters,
We toast with soda, our funny creators.
With harmonies weaving, our spirits parade,
In the melodies of laughter, love is made!

The Gift of Presence

In the land of nods and cheerful cheer,
I brought my jokes, but forgot my gear.
With silly faces and stories galore,
We giggled until we rolled on the floor.

A knock, knock joke meets a lost sock tale,
The best of presents from the wiggly whale.
We cherish each moment, oh what a scene,
Like a clumsy penguin, awkward and keen!

With pies that flop and cakes that fall,
We toast each mishap, we're having a ball.
For in this space where we truly jest,
The gift of our presence is simply the best!

So grab your hat, let's don our best smiles,
We'll spread the joy across endless miles.
In the giggles and jests, life's lively event,
In the gift of each other, our hearts are content!

Layers of Generous Hearts

Beneath our layers like a cake gone awry,
We scoop out love, oh my, oh my!
With sprinkles of kindness and frosting of fun,
We share the laughs, and no one's outdone.

Like a burrito stuffed with extra delight,
We wrap our hearts, oh what a sight!
In each silly layer, a giggle, a wink,
As we ponder the snacks that we share and think.

We peel back the layers, reveal what we love,
In this goofy gathering, we rise above.
With jests and cheer, we nurture our part,
In every bite, the dance of the heart.

So take a layer from this hefty slice,
Join in the fun; everything's nice.
For in this zany layer cake scene,
We find the joy in all that's unseen!

Stories Woven in Kindness

In a town so small, laughter flies,
A cat wore a hat, to everyone's surprise.
The baker gave bread, and a sweet pie too,
While dancers tripped over their own two.

Old Joe found a dollar, thought it was grand,
He bought a balloon that slipped from his hand.
It flew to a kid, who let out a cheer,
And soon all the neighbors joined in the beer.

A swap of the stories that made hearts glow,
The fish passed a tale, of a party in flow.
The spruced-up pine tree hummed tunes of delight,
While squirrels did the tango, a marvelous sight.

So gather your friends, and chuckle aloud,
For kindness is silly, and makes us all proud.
Share a joke or a smile, let the giggles spread,
In this wacky world, we're all better fed.

Serendipity of Sharing

A man baked a cake while wearing a frown,
But his cat was the chef, and he wore a white gown.
A whisk in one paw, with sprinkles galore,
They invited the neighbors, who banged on the door.

They danced on the table, with forks like swords,
While the cake got devoured, with plenty of chords.
Old ladies sang loud, while grandpas did jig,
Who knew sharing cake could be such a gig?

The mailman dropped muffins that he stole from a plate,
He ran past the dogs at an unbelievable rate.
Each bite that they took turned a grin ever wide,
In a feast of pure joy, we all took a ride.

So raise up your glasses, toast kindness in jest,
For sharing is messy, but brings out the best.
Laughs mixed with sugar, it's a beautiful blend,
A sprinkle of joy that just won't ever end.

Blooming in Blessings

In a garden of laughs, the flowers all chatter,
A cactus named Frank fell in love with a batter.
He said to the daisies, "Let's plant some pies!"
As the tulips concocted their high-flying lies.

The veggies teamed up for a grand parade,
With carrots in tutus, their dance not delayed.
They twirled on the grass, till they all fell down,
We cheered and we clapped for the veggie-town crown.

A gopher with glasses sold tickets to fun,
He ran through the rows, calling, "Two for one!"
Each laugh sprouted leaves, with roots deep in cheer,
In a symphony of blossoms, laughter drew near.

So plant your good deeds, let their roots intertwine,
In the soil of goodwill, let hearts brightly shine.
Those blooms of connection, both quirky and sweet,
Remind us that laughter makes life extra neat.

The Alchemy of Caring

A wizard named Fred brewed soup with a grin,
He mixed up the laughter with a dash of kin.
Each bowl that he served, brought winks and glee,
Now the squirrels had favorites as quick as could be.

The magic of sharing sparkled in sight,
As bunnies would barter for laughs every night.
With jokes on the side, they'd feast with delight,
Stirring joy in the pot till it smelled just right.

One day a raccoon, a thief with some flair,
Stole cookies left out, but we didn't care.
He danced on the bench, wore a crown made of leaves,
As everyone joined in, with chuckles and sleeves.

So gather your friends, mix the moments so bold,
For caring is funny, and that's worth its gold.
Life's recipe's rich, with laughter to share,
In the alchemy of caring, there's magic in the air.

Milton Keynes UK
Ingram Content Group UK Ltd.
UKHW021953151124
451186UK00007B/223